Time, ONLY TIME

OTHER BOOKS BY THIS AUTHOR

- **GUILT FACTORS – Mind Games & Thought Notes!**
  "A poetic & artistic adventure into the known & the unknown"

- **LOST IN THE DARKNESS OF THOUGHT**
  "A short story with a dark poetic twist"

- **SEARCHING FOR PAPA'S STAR**
  "A short story about three grandkids & their Papa"

Time, ONLY TIME

"Poetic Rumblings"

ROBERT R. BLONDIN

Copyright © 2019 by Robert R. Blondin.

All rights reserved. No part of this publication may be reproduced, distributed, or transmitted in any form or by any means, including photocopying, recording, or other electronic or mechanical methods, without the prior written permission of the publisher, except in the case of brief quotations embodied in critical reviews and certain other noncommercial uses permitted by copyright law. For permission requests, write to the publisher, addressed "Attention: Permissions Coordinator," at the address below.

ARPress
45 Dan Road Suite 36
Canton MA 02021

Hotline: 1(800) 220-7660
Fax: 1(855) 752-6001

Ordering Information:
Quantity sales. Special discounts are available on quantity purchases by corporations, associations, and others. For details, contact the publisher at the address above.

Printed in the United States of America.

ISBN-13: Hardcover   979-8-89356-069-5
          eBook   979-8-89356-070-1

Library of Congress Control Number: 2024904000

TABLE OF CONTENTS

Dedication 1
Preface 2
Time, Only Time (Part One) 4
Time, Only Time (Part Two) 6
The Pain 8
Unseen Scars 10
What My Eyes See 12
If the Morning Doesn't Come 14
Shadow of Darkness 16
Beyond the Unknown 18
Shadow of Fear 20
Silent Waves 22
Love Can Hurt 24
The Visitors 26
My Brother and I 28
The Reflection 30
The Depths of Your Mind 32
From Beyond 34
Visions Drifting Through 36
Envision Me 38
Love's Pain 40
Fears Within (Part One) 42
Fears Within (Part Two) 44
Just A Face 46

Only You Can	48
The Cottage	50
Some Kind of High	52
Why?	54
Fortunate to be One	56
A Ray of Hope	58
Temper, Temper	60
Down and Out	62
For You I'll Wait	64
That Feeling	66
Return Journey	68
Home	70
Confusion?	72
Life or Death?	74
Wanting Her	76
A Touch of Golden	78
In Memory	80

DEDICATION

"Dedicated to family & friends"

A special shout out to my children, **Kyle** (Jessica) & **Melinda** (Bruzlin), and to my grandchildren - **Austin**, **Sydney Marie**, **Jake** & **Nathaniel** (as pictured below) - *and to those that may follow!*

And to my late wife, **Marie** – R.I.P.

"Time, only time, 'til we meet again"

PREFACE

"Poetic Rumblings": a collection of free verse poems – most of which were written during the 1970's & 1980's - my personal ramblings about life, its good days and bad days, with all its misunderstandings, mishaps and other unfortunate happenings and delves into the darkness, the past and the future.

Or, the meanings of each poem can be whatever you believe it to be!?

The title of this book is based on the very first poem you'll read, but it also is so titled because it reflects the time and era these poems were in fact written.

Of course, It can also be interpreted as to how one, with luck and good health, gracefully ages over time – after all, time is ongoing and constant - time, only time. (refer to dual photo at the end, a young vs old, the aging of time itself!)

The abstract picture at the beginning is of two of my grandkids walking and holding hands (cousins Sydney Marie and Nathaniel) and to me represents going forward, advancing in life, taking the path destiny has chosen for you, or maybe the predetermined path you have duly or unduly carved out for yourself, with both positive and negative factors encompassing your being, your soul, all while you travel through time and this thing we call life.

Or, maybe it simply implies that when facing difficult times and having your backs to the wall, you cope and manage to walk away, onward and forward, with your heads held high, having overcome the challenges you may have faced.

But, again, and more importantly, as with the poems contained herein, it is your interpretation that really matters.

Time, only time, unstoppable, ongoing and persistent.

Nothing but time, until…

TIME, ONLY TIME
(PART ONE)

Nothing but time,
a circular motion in life,
changing and rearranging,
laying here awaiting my destiny.

Caressing each breath I have left,
still hoping for more,
nothing but time, only time;
now feeling my body rise and soar,
just awaiting an end.

Cylinders of darkness, tunnels of light,
peaking to the inevitable,
a circular motion of life,
nothing but time, only time.

Seconds pass, then,
the sound of broken glass,
maybe the shattering of time,
inflicting a sharp jagged pain,
leaving an aching in my heart,
that just won't pass.

Nothing but time, only time.

TIME, ONLY TIME
(PART TWO)

Falling into slow motion,
Into utter darkness, with a sudden thud,
caught in the hands of time,
unable to converse,
now charred with fear; then,
the sounds of footsteps near.

Cylinders of darkness, tunnels of light,
spiraling shadows, in and out of sight.

I'm surrounded by an aura,
a mysterious aura, with a distinct smell,
like the scent of fresh cut flowers, yet,
encircling the presence of fear,
not sure if it's the entrance to heaven or hell.

But, still, I remain here, in this world,
bound by time, nothing but time.

Time, only time.

THE PAIN

Peace is but the subsiding of pain …

Hurt is but the creation of guilt …

Guilt is but only a feeling …

Deep within the subconscious being.

UNSEEN SCARS

Childish schemes, scattered dreams,
everlasting feelings, unseen scars,
still dormant in the dark canyons of my mind,
slowly garnered, through the ages of time.

A stretching imagination, infectious in itself,
now scattered and running amok,
my spirit slightly numbed.

Deep feelings emerging,
surfacing, dangling and dancing,
as if jumping from an old dusty book.

Emotions on top of other emotions,
sometimes cascading into downright chaos,
deep dark feelings, harvested over time,
yet, harnessed over time.

Childish schemes, scattered dreams,
everlasting feelings, unseen scars.

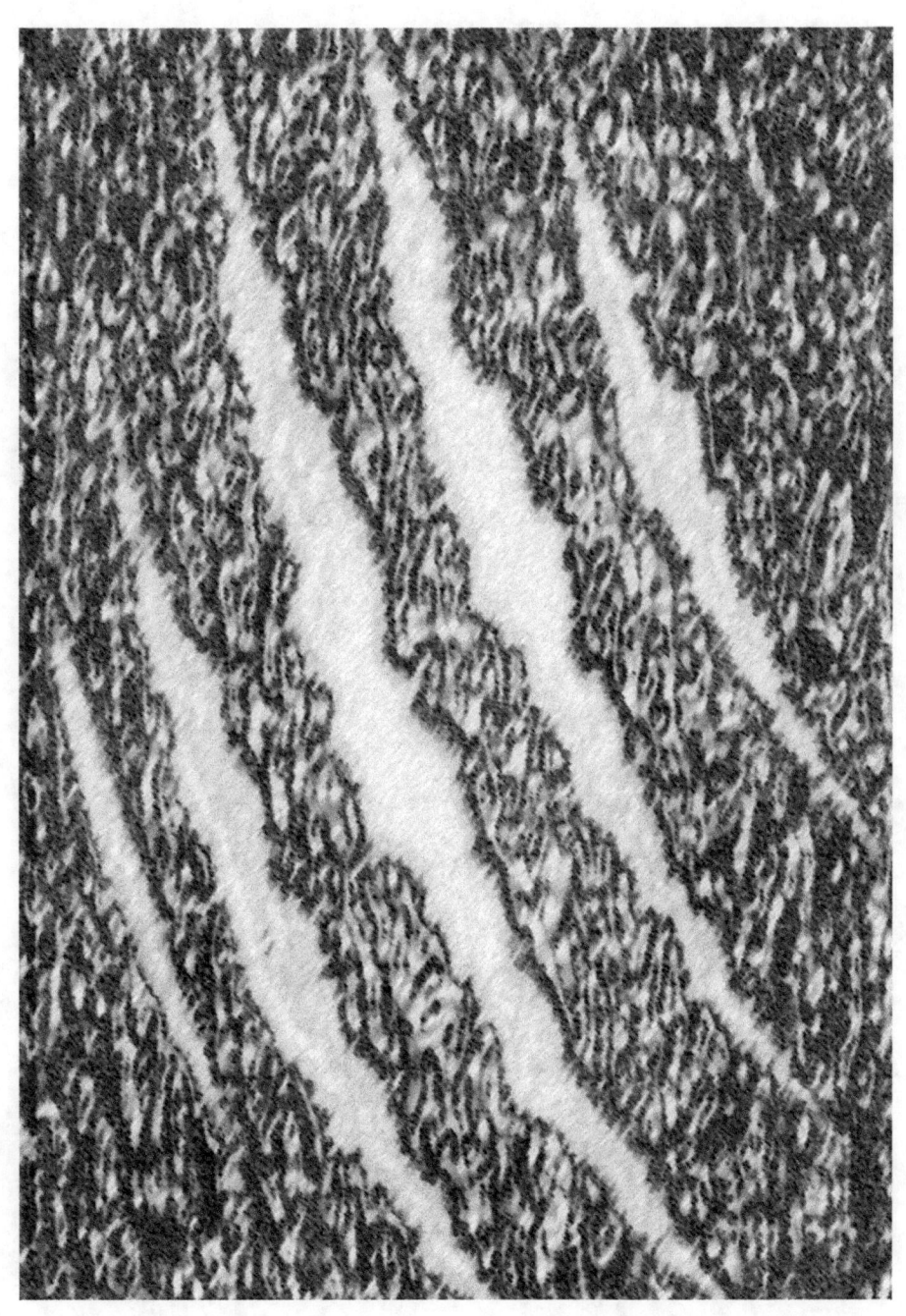

WHAT MY EYES SEE

*I shall always cry,
because my eyes see life as a lie.*

*Each sorrow or great happiness,
is only what we scrounge, beg or borrow.*

*To live a life is not to rest,
beyond is what we shall truly live.*

*I foresee a wondrous and glorious sight,
pure, crystal and natural as light.*

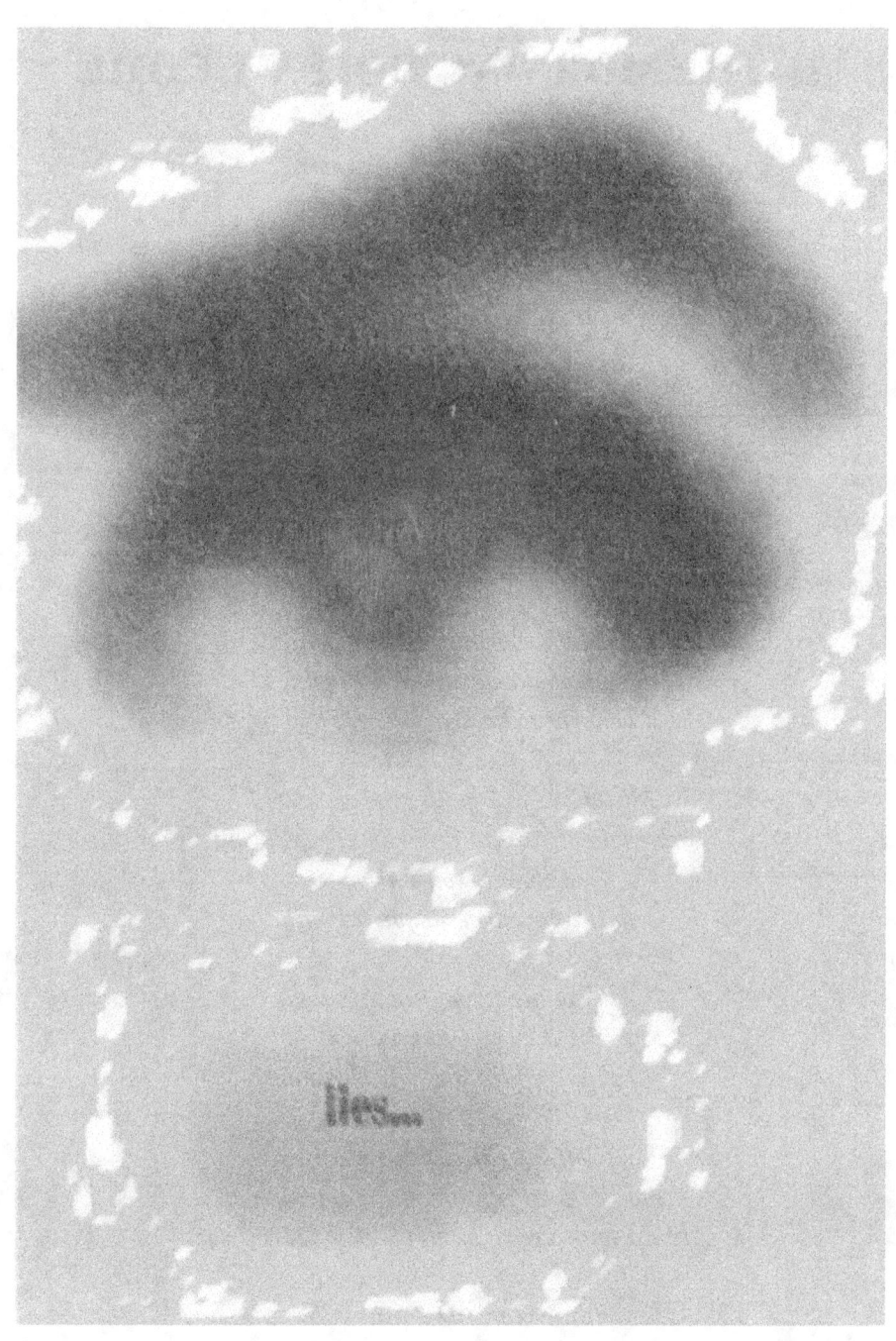

IF THE MORNING DOESN'T COME

If the morning doesn't come,
and your day turns to night,
I'll be there to make it alright.

If you're down and lonely,
and the feeling of life has gone,
I'll be over to sing a sweet song.

If your heart becomes broken,
and you need soft words spoken,
I'll be there, 'cause I care.

If your morning doesn't come,
and your day turns to night,
I'll be there to hold you close, oh so tight.

If you see your path getting weary,
and you don't quite know what you'll find,
I'll show you the way,
for I am yours and you are mine.

If you need love and affection,
I'll be your connection,
I'll put you in the right direction.

If you can't find what you seek,
and darkness fills the air, stay with me,
I'll help you search, you know how much I care.

If the morning doesn't come
and your day turns to night,
I'll always be there, making it alright.

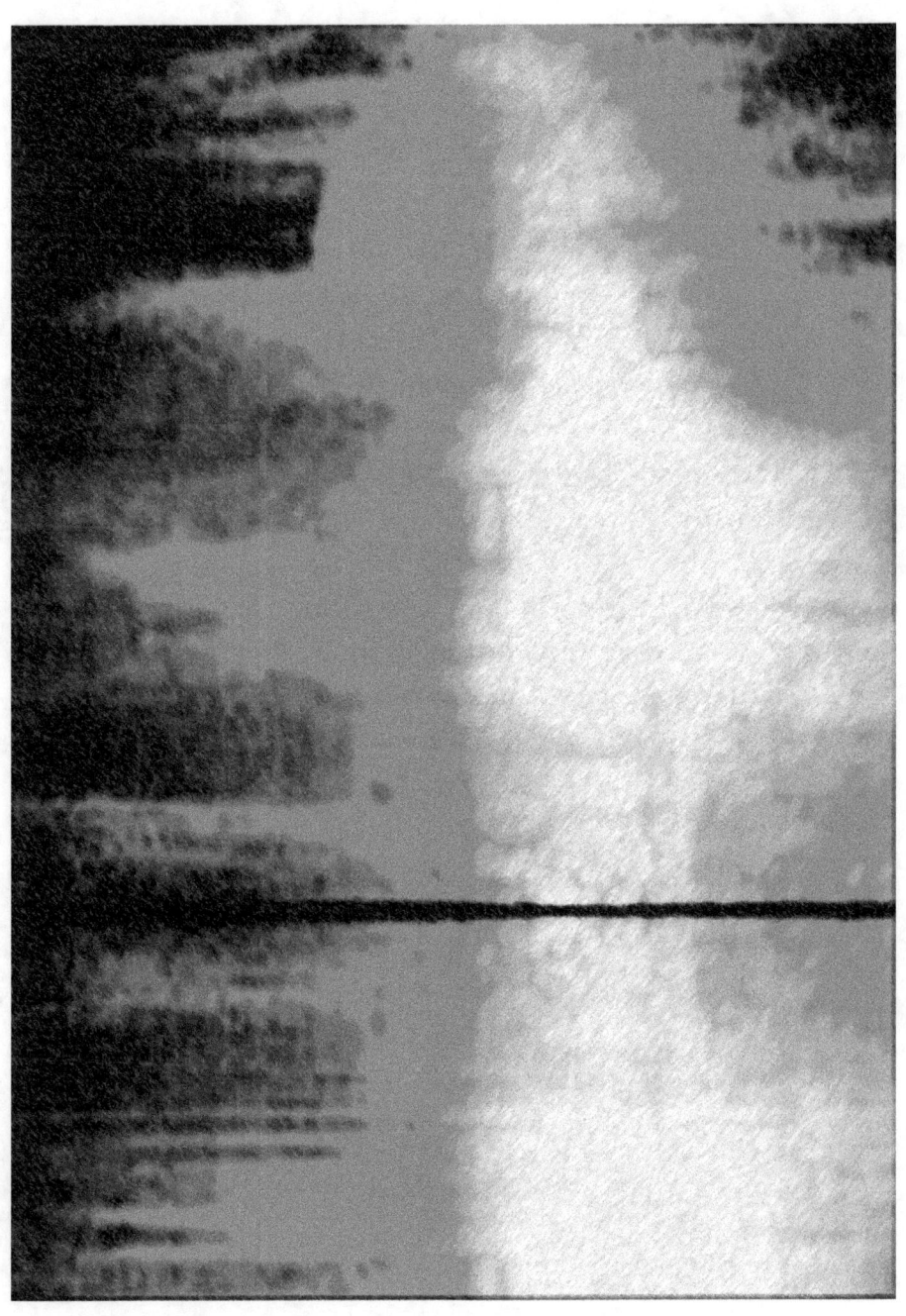

SHADOW OF DARKNESS

The forthcoming of darkness,
the coming of death,
gliding slowly down the trail,
searching for my place of rest.

Just floating through the lonely,
gloomy and dank secluded passages,
as the dark stillness closes in.

My memories slowly emerge,
going back and forth in time,
seeing what I've done, where I've been;
all fading from the sublime, to blackness and back again,
then, the shadow of darkness,
... of death!

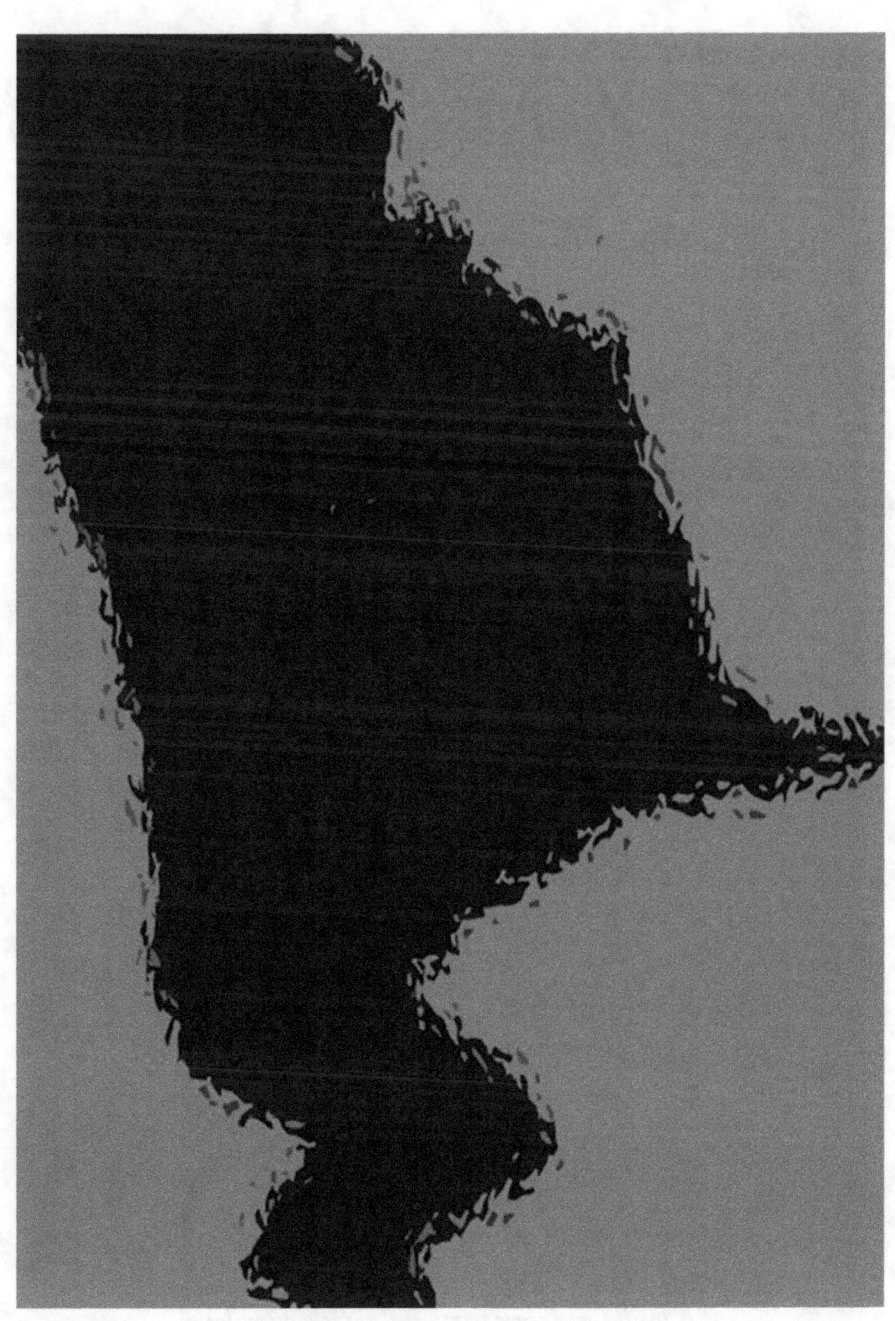

BEYOND THE UNKNOWN

Reasoning beyond doubt,
outer limits unseen,
inner planetary objects,
swirling and jutting out.

The dark horizons yet unearthed,
ghastly experiments being secretly researched,
all wondering who will be first.

The forthcoming of light,
the utter darkness of night,
with creations beyond thought,
the world as it is and is not.

Amazed and bewildered at how it all began,
the so-called evolution of modern day man,
does anyone really know,
can anyone even begin to understand?

This world of ours just keeps growing and growing,
populations exploding, volcanos erupting,
rivers and oceans overflowing,
and nobody really knowing.

Although the great book has been written,
the real truth, the only truth, is not known,
or is it all just fabrication and totally overblown.

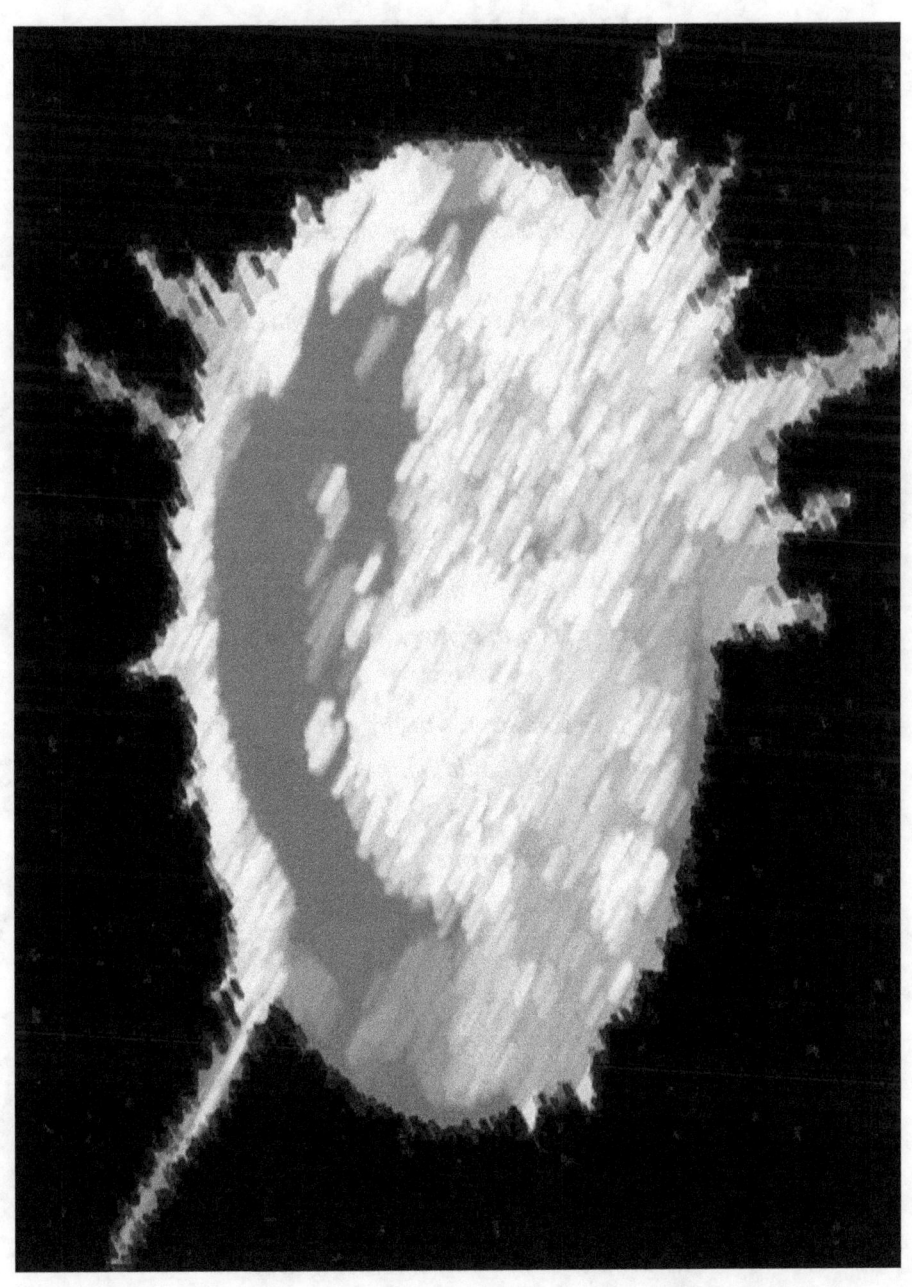

SHADOW OF FEAR

Her eyes were a glittering green, with a bewildering gleam,
and her hair was a golden hue, but so damp,
with a light touch of early morning dew.

She stood in a shadow of her own making,
as if there for the taking.

The air had a scent of the wild, but yet,
with a temperament, quite mild.

She raised her hand, motioning me forward;
I made a step, but froze, like a coward.

I could sense an evil near, but my eyes could not see,
and I could not hear.

I felt the excitement she created,
the thrill she instilled in me.

She was a silhouette outline, in the narrow path ahead,
her piercing eyes paralyzing me; all my senses now dead.

Unconsciously I approached, with a cautious step,
I knew I could not turn back, not now, not ever, not yet.

Her arms stretched out, embracing my soul,
my anticipation grew, and then withdrew, and then,
everything went cold, she had hold.

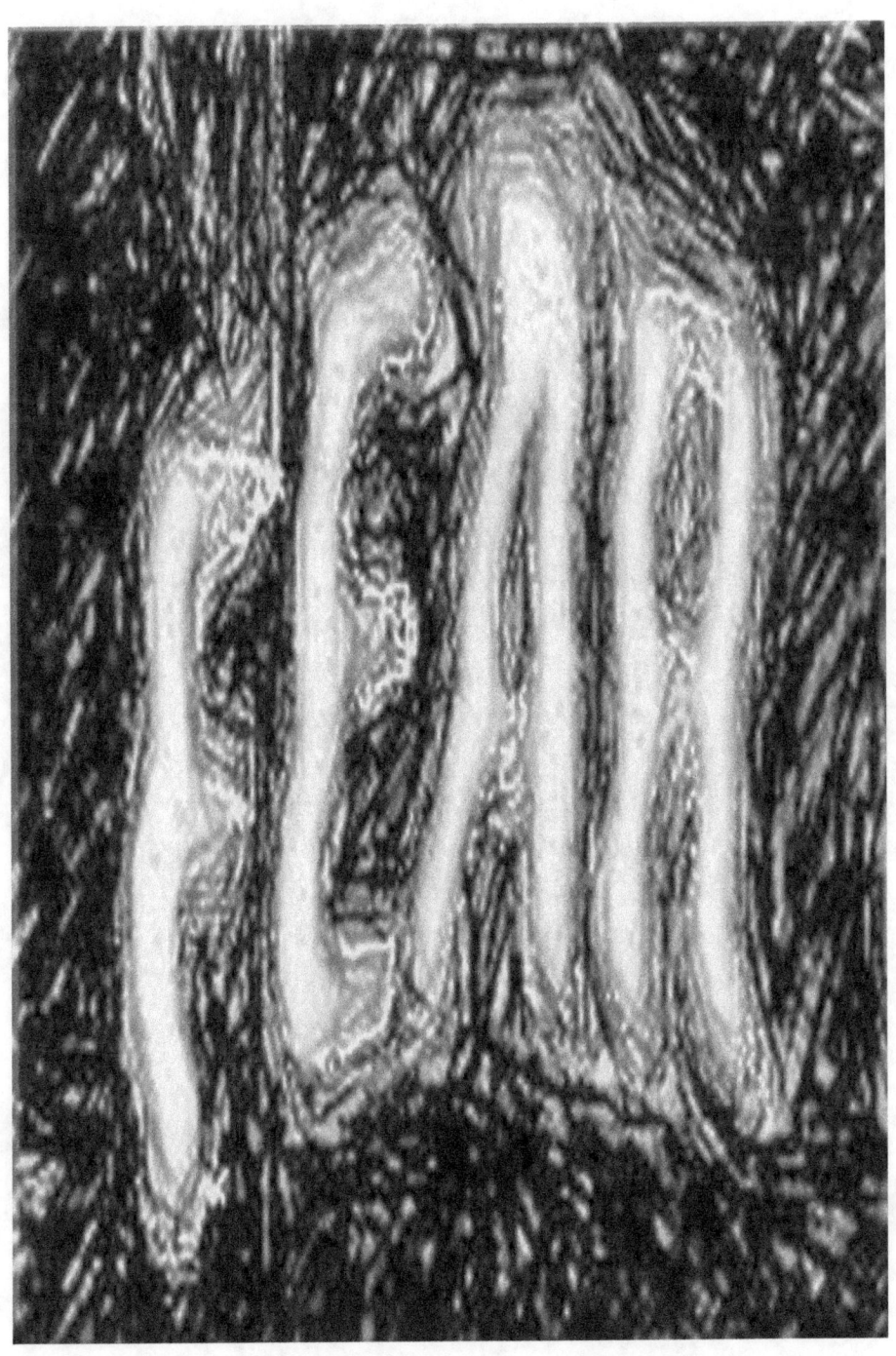

SILENT WAVES

Silent waves, the solemn soft wind blowing,
clear blue water flowing.

Seeing a vision of her on the sandy shore,
but now disappearing,
to be seen no more.

Suddenly a nasty cool wind appears,
creating a fortress in the sand;
and from the formed gritty mound,
comes the formation of a hand,
stretching and reaching out,
grasping for fulfillment.

Fear instills my already trembling body,
as the hand surges upward and forward,
slowly approaching my soul,
coming closer, closer, and closer,
grasping for a piece of me,
a small piece of reality.

An inner sense suddenly emerges
and destroys my thinking,
both reality and non-reality now linking,
as I open my eyes to the silent waves,
and the solemn soft wind blowing.

LOVE CAN HURT

Never would I ever,
fall in love again,
never would I ever,
glance at your picture again,
it's hidden in a drawer,
to be seen no more.

I loved you so much,
to caress, hold and touch.

Your loving smile, your kiss,
so luscious, but yet amiss,
and all the while,
you left leaving me in vain,
driving me to go slowly insane.

Never would I ever,
fall in love again,
never would I ever,
glance at your picture again.

No valid reasons given,
you just up and went;
so what's the purpose of living,
my times all used, all spent;
never would I ever,
fall in love again.

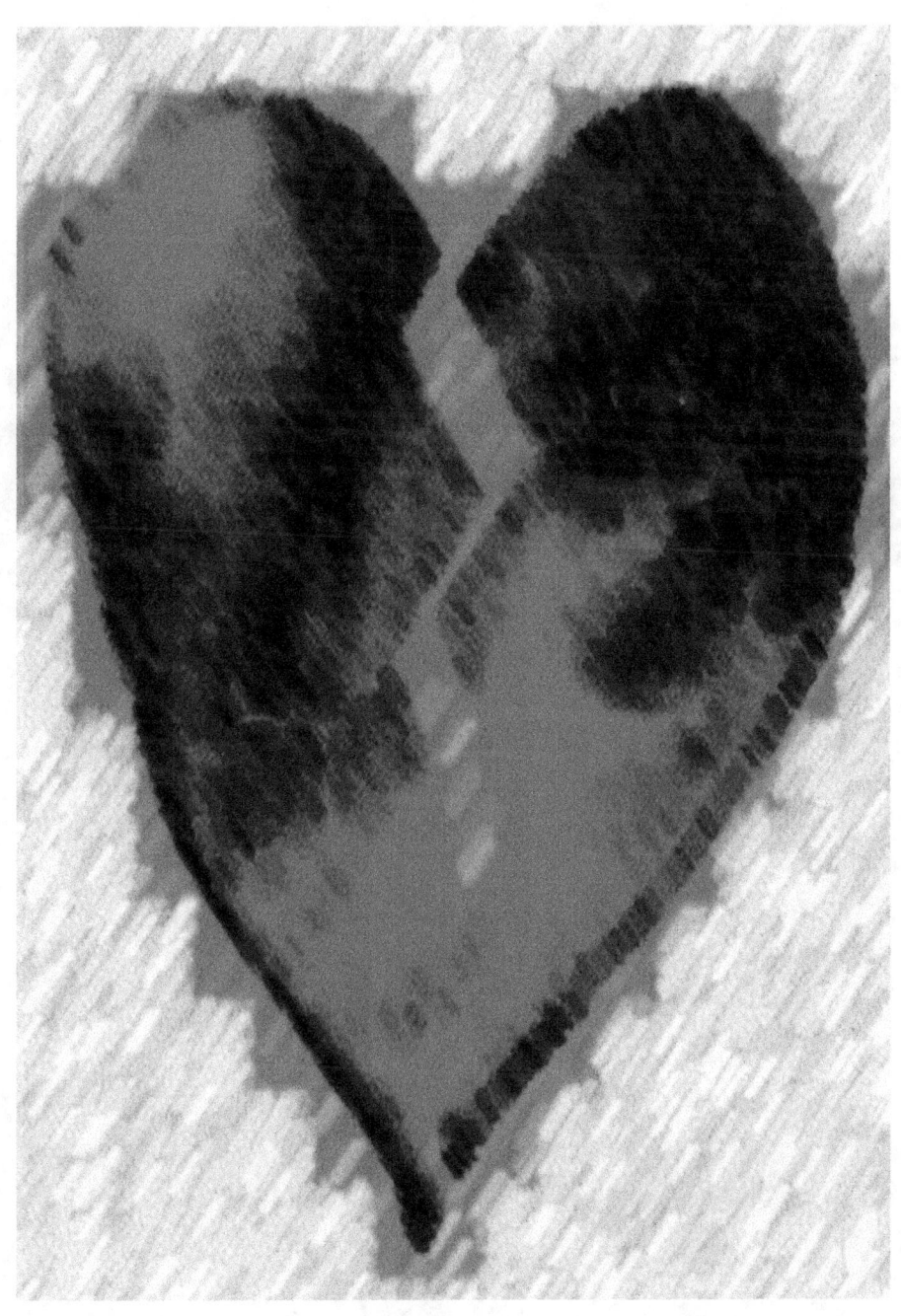

THE VISITORS

We come to you in thoughts,
sometimes quickly, sometimes not.

We stay as long as we want,
or, as long as you want.;
we sometimes even haunt,
maybe just taunt.

We survive in memories, good or bad,
you control the emotion,
whatever the notion,
it's not a magic potion.

We sometimes appear as magical orbs,
sometimes shadows, white or black,
just to give you a shivering flashback.

We come to you in thoughts,
sometimes quickly, sometimes not.

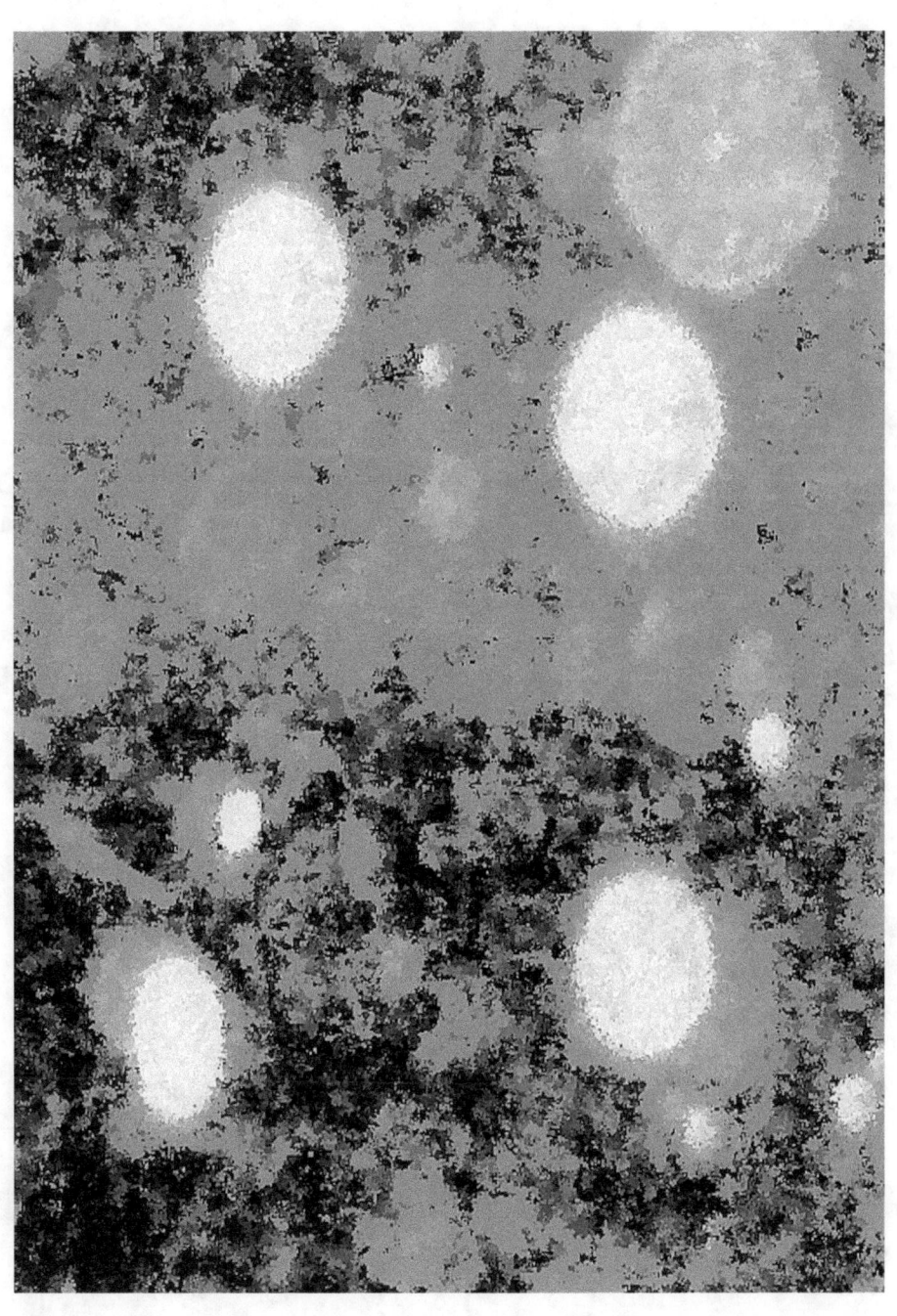

MY BROTHER AND I …

My brother and I …
Only heaven keeps us parted;
but somehow I feel restrained,
and still I remain, here where I started.

Being one with one is not to run;
look into my eyes for I'm no spy;
and, if you should cry, you'll realize why,
be calm my brother, to me we'll live forever.

Greeting is our eternal gift,
goodbye is nothing to our mind's eye,
love is what holds us together;
we'll meet again, only to begin.

Yes, my brother, to begin.

THE REFLECTION

Into a mirror I gaze,
the lone figure drifting into haze,
a reflection of life;
the dark image comes into view,
that image of death itself.

The innerness of my being,
touching, clutching my very soul;
the reflection surges forward,
standing out like it was borrowed;
visualizing into life, into utter realization.

With one last hope of courage,
I reach to destroy it,
that dark reflective image,
but as my flesh touches the cold aura,
a flashing bright haloed light shines and emerges,
emitting the final calling.

THE DEPTHS OF YOUR MIND

Drifting fever of love, everlasting feelings,
through the weathered ages of time,
holding onto only a fraction that is mine.

Awaiting the deafening sound,
yet to hear and find,
knowing the thunderous shaking,
the pounding in your mind.

Widening landscapes of the universe,
unkind and treacherous people,
all just making it worse.

Your stretching imagination running away,
deep within the non-reality of thought,
seeing the world as it is and is not,
happiness, wistfulness,
and then, the silence,
the unsaid death.

To be at peace within the saneness of life,
the reality of being, the true reality of life;
sometimes the answer is just too hard,
too tough to find, knowing the guilt,
the guilt within the depths of your mind.

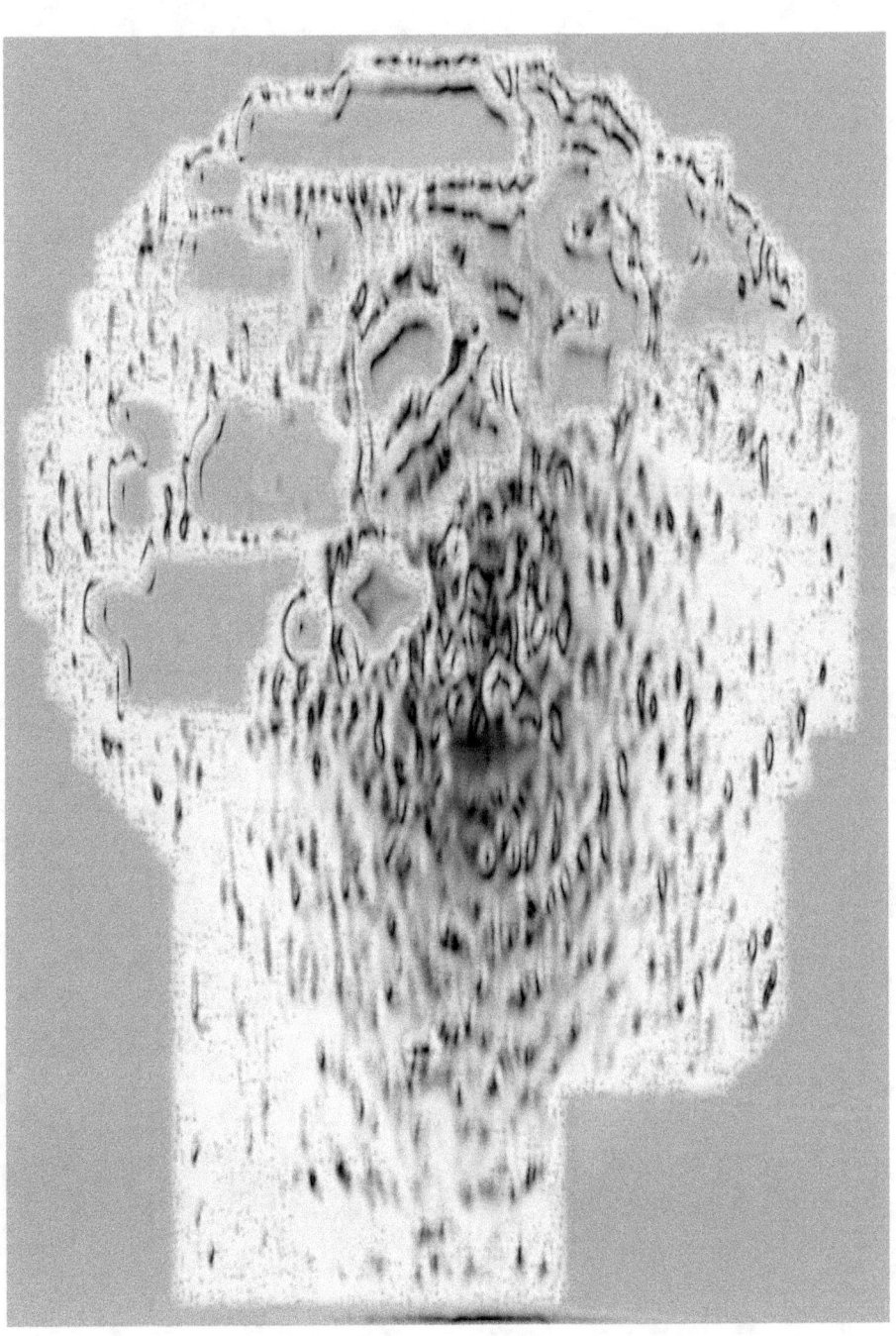

FROM BEYOND

Beckoning calls from beyond,
the deafening screeching noise,
engulfing my soul, my mind,
my golden silence now gone.

The shrieking noise thrusts forward,
reaching out, clutching, wrestling,
slicing through the thin air;
the ensuing gust turns me about;
leaving me in hopeless despair.

Within the whispers of the cool breeze,
I can hear the sounds imposing,
the beckoning sounds enclosing,
those shuttering calls from beyond,
such an eerie feeling, an eerie tone,
my senses all gone, now all alone.

VISIONS DRIFTING THROUGH

*Your face, your smile,
visions drifting through,
I forgot not to remember you.*

*A whispering breeze mentions your name,
slowly, agonizingly, driving me insane.*

*The beauty of your smile,
your long flowing hair,
visions drifting through,
I forgot not to remember you.*

*You're with me, inside me,
as I walk, you walk,
as I talk, you talk,
visions drifting through,
I forgot not to remember you.*

*Your loveliness caresses my soul,
as the mystics unfold,
your spiritual presence,
apparent and reaching out,
now touching, feeling, existing,
you're with me, inside me,
and all because I forgot,
I forgot not to remember you.*

ENVISION ME

Envision me,

Visualize my being,

Suspended in time,

Caress the aura,

The sensation benign,

Envision me,

Touch my soul,

Envision me,

Here I am, floating in time.

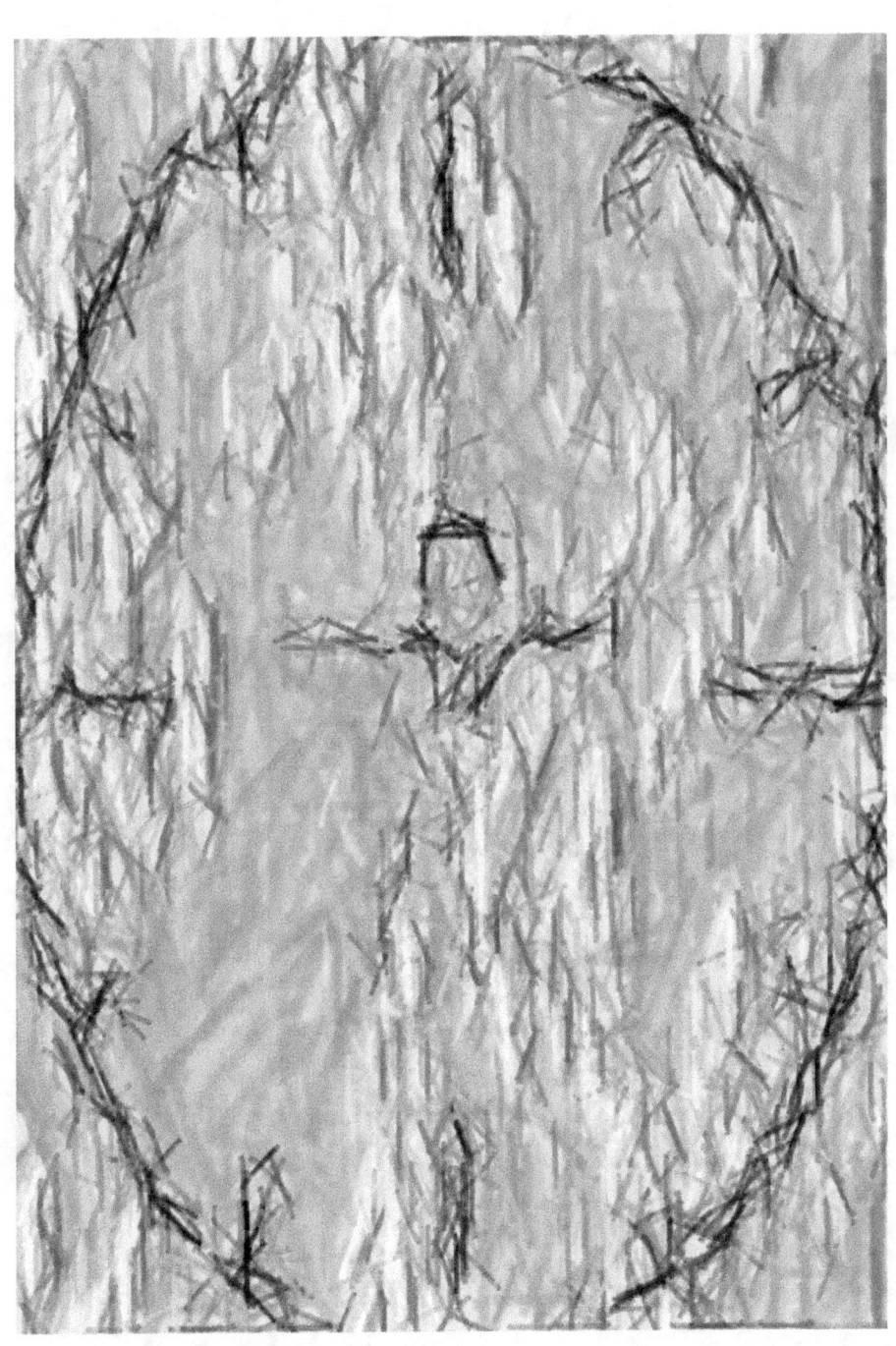

LOVE'S PAIN

*Creation is but the pain of ecstasy,
the suffering you must bear.*

*You can surely see, by eying your past,
the shame doesn't have to last and last.*

*Be at peace with thy soul;
accept, care and share.*

*Don't carry life and offer revenge,
the birth of life is what we yearn.*

*And, to err is but to learn,
nothing is quite the same as 'love's pain',
the great feeling of new life,
one within one.*

*So, don't carry life and offer revenge,
your actions were but hardcore dramatics,
an immature reason for getting your kicks.*

*Reach out for a warm hand,
an understanding heart,
you might just find a kind and gentle soul.*

Don't carry life and yet offer revenge.

And who am I? I'm but a friend!

FEARS WITHIN
(PART ONE)

The danger erupts,
the unknown thrusts forward;
the invisible twine, entangling,
tightening, choking, strangling,
gasping for air, all in utter despair.

Fears within;
the unknown remains unknown!

Wanting the simple truth,
craving the inevitable,
seeking the realism of life,
the awakening of life,
searching for a true tomorrow,
the future of mankind.

Fears within;
the unknown remains unknown!

Does it?

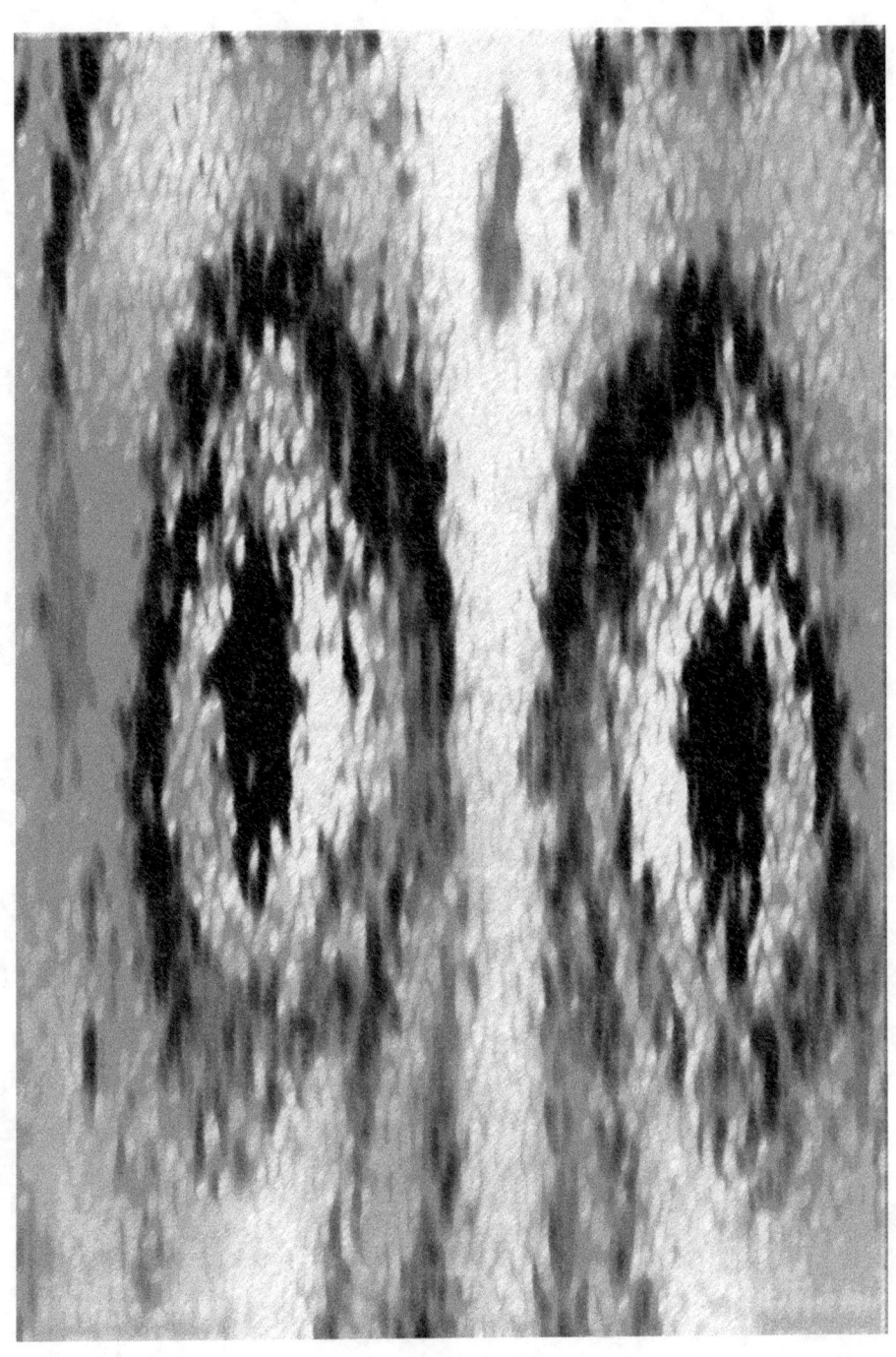

FEARS WITHIN
(PART TWO)

Reaching into the emptiness,
the openness of outer space,
editing tomorrow's headlines,
knowing the unsaid predictions,
seeing errors not yet made.

Fears within;
the unknown remains unknown!

Watching life's tragic trail,
a heart stopping fail;
hearing earthquakes not yet erupting,
speaking words not yet known,
or never ever spoken;
feeling the pain still to be felt.

Fears within;
the unknown remains unknown!

Does it?

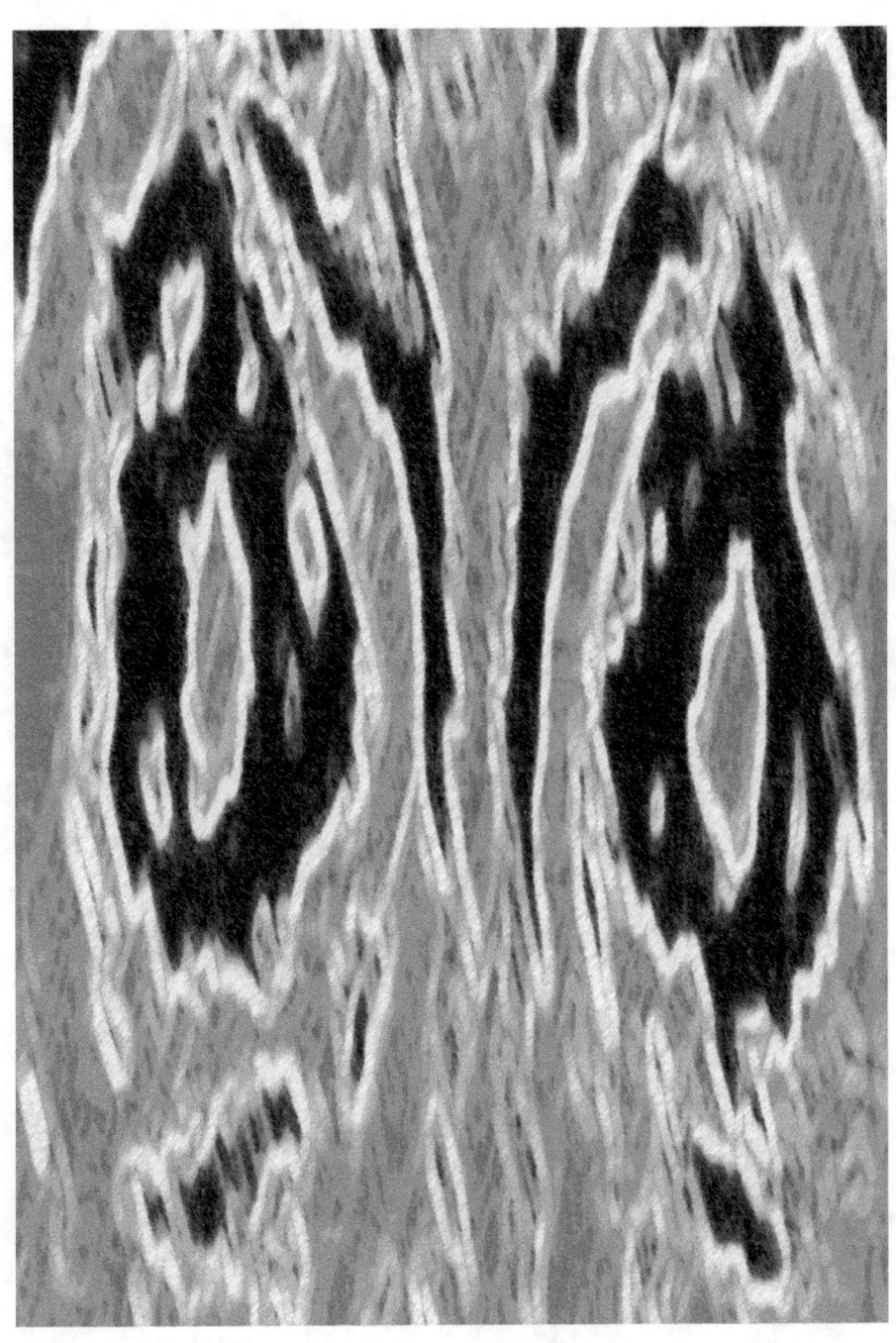

JUST A FACE

Within a mirror you see but a face,
within your mind not a trace,
the reverse reflection does not reveal,
the blank picture of how you really feel.

Seeing a vision of nothing living,
no sense of what the image is giving.

It's just a face, without a trace,
amid a glancing look into space.

Into the mirror you visualize,
take a closer look, maybe you'll realize.

Seeing a vision of nothing living,
just a face, just a face,
your outlook so misguided,
maybe just out-of-place,
such an utter waste.

ONLY YOU CAN

I have seen the sign,
seen your kind,
nothing will stop me now.

I have felt the hurt,
felt my face ground into dirt,
nothing will stop me now.

I have known your likes
and your dislikes, known
how high you set your sights,
nothing will stop me now.

I have been there before,
been able to face the chore,
nothing will stop me now.

I have known the sensations,
known the provocations,
nothing will stop me now.

I have known love,
known how it is to be well above,
nothing will stop me now.

No, nothing will stop me now.

Only you can.

THE COTTAGE

Trees swaying in the cool breeze,

branches staying in tune with the leaves;

nearby, a little brook calmly flowing,

along the side, wild flowers growing,

the surroundings enhanced with love,

expectations far and above,

time for seclusion without confusion,

the cottage, a nice location,

with no provocation.

SOME KIND OF HIGH

Perspective dreams,
with cowardly schemes.

Sudden characteristics changing,
with lives shuffled and rearranging.

Pictorial patterns, filled with golden Saturns,
and pixilated people vividly feeble.

Just fabrications of mine,
concepts and visual memories,
caught up in a quandary of time,
and so drastically benign.

Oh, it was some kind of high!

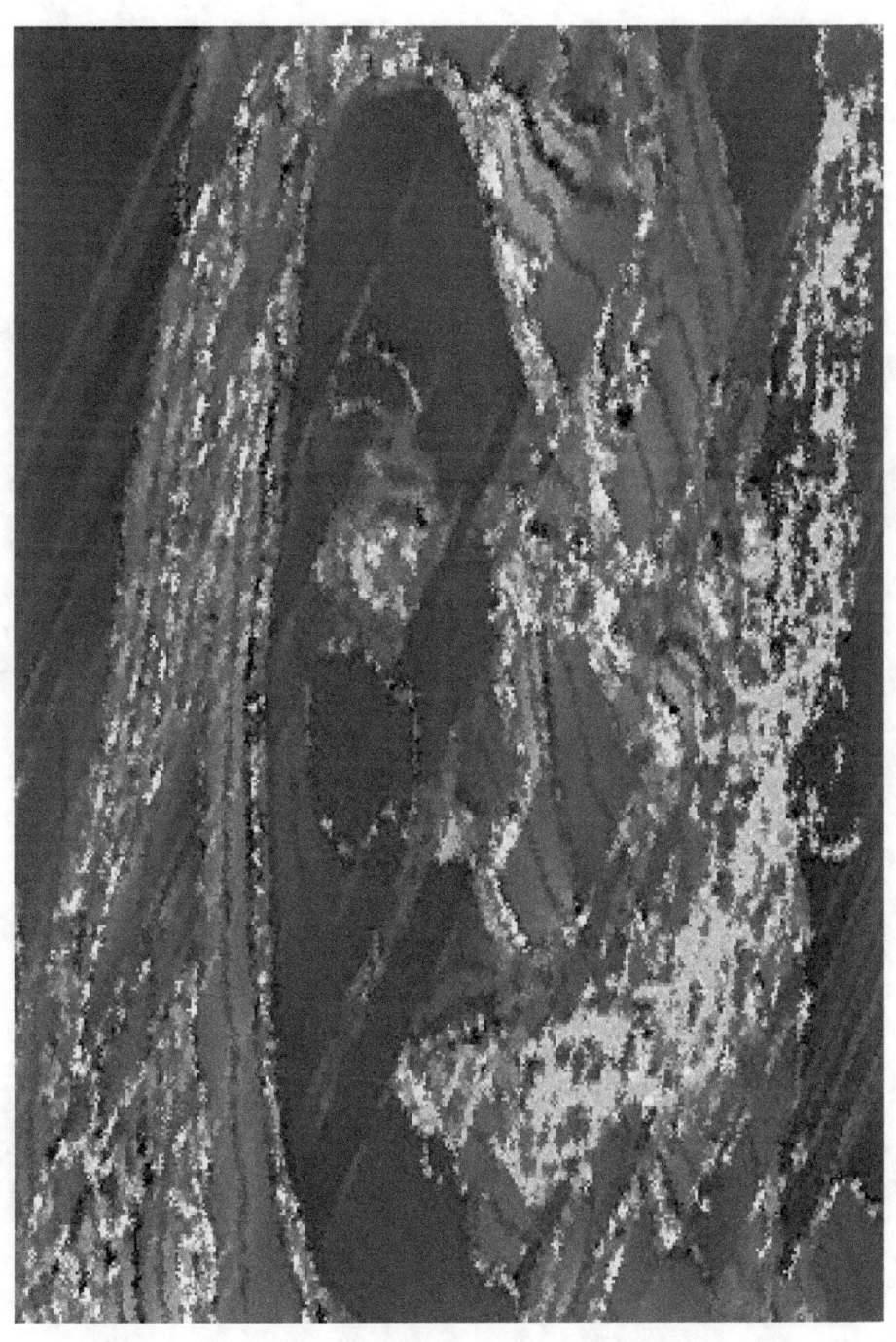

WHY?

*Inner feelings creeping,
loving tears seeping,
glaring, glimmering eyes upon you,
holding back the tears,
for a man does not cry,
don't ask the reasons why,
it's something grown in a man,
since way back when.*

*A man's feelings should never be expressed,
never second-guessed;
a leader and protector he must be,
the tears we should not see,
for if he does weep and cry,
he must give excuses, reasons why.*

*Inner feelings creeping,
loving eyes seeping,
glaring eyes upon you.*

... why?

FORTUNATE TO BE ONE

Times are hard and times are tough,
be happy you've got more than some,
yet, wishing and hoping for more,
but no one ever has enough,
be fortunate to be one.

To be one with one is not to run,
you're damn fortunate to be one.

With this ever changing world we live in,
your life will keep rearranging,
melodies will keep playing,
so just reach for the utmost,
just be yourself,
and, remember, don't boast,
just relax, just coast.

People make their own lives,
with Fathers, Mothers, Sons and Daughters,
Husbands and Wives;
so to be one with one is not to run,
you're fortunate to be one.

Your life is your life,
but don't forget, others have a share,
so don't take it away,
others care, they really do care.

To be one with one is not to run,
yes, you're damn fortunate to be one!

A RAY OF HOPE

In the mysterious depths of my mind,
its wondrous spirits fly.

My consciousness reaps and sows,
my mind absorbs the tolls,
my soul hides deep, does not sleep.

I stay withdrawn, something is gnawing,
yet I feel it's presence known,
something is glowing.

It's very brief and brilliant ray,
tells me that my world is surely okay!

TEMPER, TEMPER

*So calm and sentimental I tried to be,
but it surged forward, started strangling me.*

*The guilt I had inside, too hard to conceal;
emotional outbursts, loss of control,
no longer did I have a sense of real.*

What is this, what do I feel?

*It gushed outwardly, flowing quite free,
nothing can stop the onslaught;
maybe only me.*

*It heaped to the top, hot, hot, hot,
it would not be suppressed,
it could not be stopped.*

Temper, temper.

DOWN AND OUT

Another day of utter loneliness,
nothing ever going right;
it can all be said by the stillness,
the silence of the night.

Here I am, down and out,
absolutely no doubt,
I don't know what it's all about.

Seeing visions of nothing, hearing
whispered words spoken, feeling
down and quite heartbroken.

The subdued aura, the quietness,
the silence inflicting my mind,
I'm pondering over what's to be,
what's left behind?

Here I am, down and out,
clearly no doubt,
I don't know what it's all about.

FOR YOU I'LL WAIT

*A song in my heart
and no one to listen.*

*Longing, waiting and hoping,
and for what?*

*I'm empty, I'm still,
my heart keeps pounding,
feelings running adrift.*

*Visions sad and visions glad;
not sure what I have,
what I might have had.*

Where am I? What am I?

*Here alone, not quite content,
hollow, incomplete and spent.*

*Bring to me the one I love,
we'll sing our love song,
until the day we're gone.*

*Hold me, touch me,
breathe for me, with me,
caress my soul, be with me.*

*For you I'll wait,
my strength is great.*

THAT FEELING

*To see the hurt approaching,
knowing what to expect.*

*To wander through the darkness,
to feel the never-ending pain.*

*To want what can never be yours,
to feel the sorrow once again.*

Pain ... a feeling that slowly ceases!

RETURN JOURNEY

I, the one that is born;;;

I the one that breathes;;;

I, the one that lives...

I, the one that dies...

I, the one that is reborn!

HOME

It sure wasn't much,
but we called it home,
Mom and Dad had twelve kids,
So no one was ever alone.

We all got by with what we had,
times were hard but also quite glad;
we all shared what there was,
hand-me-downs, on top of all the love.

Yes, poor we were but love was always there,
respect and admiration everywhere.

It sure wasn't much,
no prosperity as such,
but we called it home.

Mom and Dad had twelve kids,
So no one was ever alone.

CONFUSION?

From a painter's point of view,
the picture on the wall said it all.

The curves and strokes of the brush,
vibrating a titillating rush.

The vibrant color fast designs,
with protuberant lines and shades of hue,
creating a perspective quite anew

But only a case of fiction, not fact.

And, if thou art confused,
it must be abstract!!

LIFE OR DEATH?

The cutting off of Life.

The dullness of a cold shrieking knife.

The hurt, the everlasting scar.

Outdoing the pain of life by far.

WANTING HER

Where did I go wrong,
Am I not where I belong?

What has happened to my mind?
I seem to be wandering,
dreaming in a past time.

Maybe I'm just wishing,
hoping I was back there,
in a time, so young, so in love,
with the one
I cherished, far and above.

Or, am I slowly losing my mind,
sweet memories of the girl,
the love once mine.

It use to be so clear,
so vivid in my mind,
wanting her, needing her,
yet knowing I'll never have her.

Wanting her but not getting,
so long ago, all in a past time,
all within my mind.

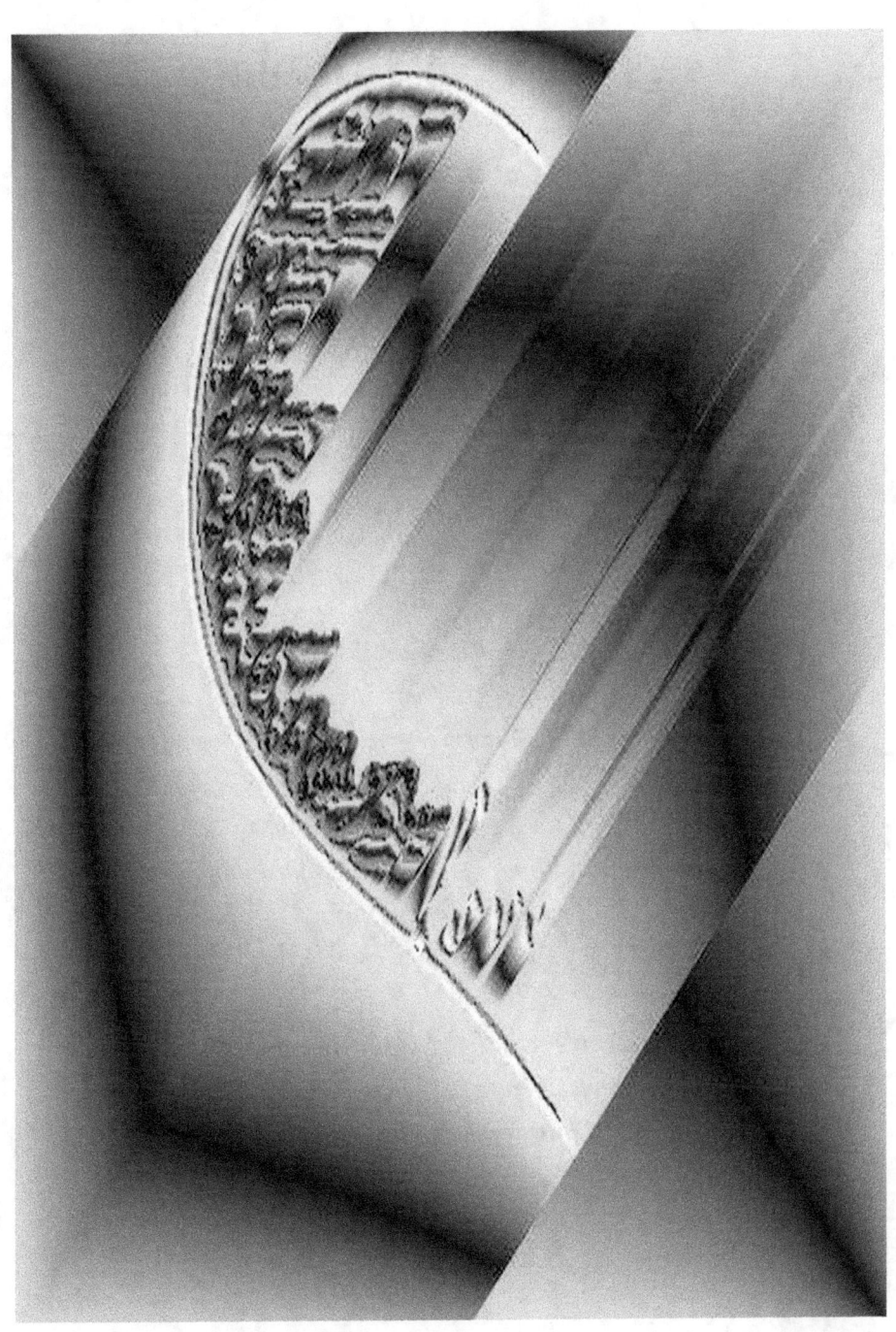

A TOUCH OF GOLDEN

(An Ode to Mom & Dad)

*Fifty years and a thousand
or so tears, are what a
wedding anniversary holds.*

*Life's been oh so wonderful,
oh so sweet.*

And, now it's a 'touch of golden'.

*Your lives have been full, oh
so complete, you've tasted
life's bittersweet melody.*

*With twelve marvelous children,
so many grandchildren and great grandchildren,
you've had God's blessing,
we've had your blessing.*

*Sweet memories of good times gone by,
remembering the downfalls too,
but cherishing it all, through and through.*

*You've made us all appreciate and understand,
the meaning of Love, the true meaning of Life.*

And, you are the Love of our Life.

*It's been a touch of golden,
yes, fifty years,
but your golden years are only about to begin.*

Yes, fifty years and a thousand or so tears.

*God Bless your anniversary and God Bless You.
I love you (we love you).*

IN MEMORY

*In loving memory of my Mom & Dad,
long gone but never forgotten.*

Evelyn & William Blondin
Callander, Ontario, Canada

TIME, ONLY TIME

"Poetic Rumblings"

Robert R. Blondin

- The End -

bobmeistersplace.com
bobmeisterb@gmail.com

www.ingramcontent.com/pod-product-compliance
Lightning Source LLC
Chambersburg PA
CBHW050249010526
44107CB00003B/252